# A Meg's Meadows Christmas

Written by

MaryAnn Myers

Sunrise Horse Farm
11872 Chillicothe Road
Chesterland, Ohio 44026
440-729-0930
www.sunrisehorsefarm.com

First Edition
10  9 8 7 6 5 4 3 2 1

1.Fiction  2.Thoroughbreds  3.Family  4.Christmas

Also by the author

~ * ~

*Call Me Lydia*
*Maple Dale*
*Favored to Win*
*Maple Dale Revisited*
*The Frog, the Wizard, and the Shrew*
*Ellie's Crows*
*Hannah's Home*
*A Thoroughbred's Dream*
*Odds on Favorite*
*Barn 14 ~ Meg's Meadows*
*Maple Dale ~ My Forever Home*
*Soon to be a Movie*
*Wire to Wire*
*Tetch*
*Ben Said*
*Fiona*
*Beau Born's Legacy*

~ * ~

*The National Weather Service classifies a storm a blizzard if it manifests large amounts of snowfall or has blowing snow in near gale-force winds. Lake Effect is a meteorological phenomenon created by the collision of Artic cold fronts sweeping generally west to east with the relatively warmer air overlying the Great Lakes. If winds are light enough to move the falling snow onshore, but not strong enough to blow the developing system over the area quickly, snowfalls measuring 4–6 feet are possible. A particularly violent storm arising from a rare combination of these adverse meteorological factors is known as a Perfect Storm.*

## Meg's Meadows Christmas

There's always a good chance of having a White Christmas in Northeast Ohio, thanks largely to Lake Effect snow. But a blizzard? A storm of that magnitude is rarer than one might think. According to meteorological statistics, there were only four actual blizzards ever reported in the area. Ben said he distinctly remembered five in his lifetime.

"The first one was when I was only four years old. My mom tied us by our waists to the bedframe and we all sat shoulder-to-shoulder waiting for the storm to pass."

Maeve, Maria, and D.R. stared wide-eyed. "Were you scared?" D.R. asked.

"No, not really. Well, maybe a little. I had no idea what a blizzard was."

"What did you think it was?"

"I don't know." Ben shrugged. "Frost built up on the inside walls and we couldn't see out the windows. But in the end, everything was okay. The storm passed and we all got a piece of licorice."

"Why?"

"For being brave I guess."

"I'm brave."

"So am I."

"Me too."

Ben smiled. "We're all going to be just fine. A blizzard is just a lot of snow and some wind."

"Besides, it's too far away to forecast the weather accurately," Señor added. "If the wind shifts even slightly...."

Tom and George agreed.

"We've had plenty of storms before."

"We're used to snow."

Marvin shook his head. "Yeah, but two feet of it in a twelve-hour period and possibly more if the wind shifts even slightly. I don't know about that."

D.R. raised his hand. "Is ninety percent a lot or a little?"

Randy looked at him. "It depends on the scale. Ninety out of a hundred is a lot. Ninety out of a thousand is not. Why? Is that for homework?"

"No." D.R. pointed to the television. "That lady just said those are the odds for the Christmas blizzard."

Everyone just looked at him for a second and then started paying attention to the TV themselves. "Turn it up." Ben said.

"From all indications, this storm is setting up to possibly be the worst this area has ever seen."

"Holy crap," Tom muttered.

"We're expecting sustained wind gusts of forty-five to fifty miles per hour and up to thirty inches of snow or more in an eight-hour period. The National Weather Bureau has upgraded the Storm Watch to a Storm Warning. By all accounts it is going to be a very memorable White Christmas. Stay tuned for further updates."

## *Four Days Before Christmas*

Everyone had their own ideas about what needed to be done to prepare for the inevitable storm. Making sure all the power generators were in good working condition was George's and Señor's primary concern. Horses could do without lights in the barn but they had to have water. The cistern would be inaccessible in a winter blizzard, so it was imperative they have a generator for each of the three barns, in addition to one for T-Bone's Place and one for Ben's farmhouse. After much discussion, they'd come to a unanimous decision to hunker down together at both places. George and Brenda and Mark and Susie were going to ride out the storm at T-Bone's with Nurse Vicky and the old-timers, and along with all the rest, Lucy, Junior, and little Julie were going to go over to Ben's. This way all the children would be able to keep one another company and Carol was planning all sorts of fun activities for them.

Nottingham Downs was closed for the winter and the General Office had shut down for the Holidays, so the plan was to try and make sure no one would have to leave the farm during the blizzard for anything, barring a veterinarian emergency. Planning and preparing for the storm was almost fun, a*lmost* being the operative word. With the elderly residents at T-Bone's Place in addition to both Ben and Dusty being well up in age, anything could happen. No one mentioned their concerns in regards to that, but it was right there front and center along with the advancing clouds in the deep blue sky. Daytime temperatures were holding in the mid-thirties along with upper-twenties at night; the ideal scenario for Lake Effect snow.

The horses were all feeling extra frisky, their winter coats puffed up, and nostrils flaring. George and Glenda and Tom and Junior had their hands full with their daily routine of getting them out to the paddocks in the morning and come dinner time, bringing them all back inside the barn. Legacy had finally settled into the farm routine. His sire, Beau Born, kept giving him the evil eye the first couple of weeks when he came home from the racetrack and the colt seemed to have been toying with the idea of taking on his old man. The two got into some major screaming and posturing matches from across the aisle of one another in the stallion barn and it was cause for a full-fledged Meg's Meadows celebration the day they finally quieted down.

Getting the weanlings out and ultimately back in required Dawn's and Lucy's assistance. It was all hands on deck. The babies were well-behaved for the most part. They'd been handled and taught to lead practically from the day they were born. But being babies there were times it was more like a circus than a parade. By far the worst was All Together's filly, and since George had to be careful with his broken-now-healed but still-sensitive leg, Tom always handled her.

Lucy loved being called on to help, as it got her out of the intense heat at T-Bone's which was kept at a constant seventy-five degrees because the overriding majority of the residents liked it that way. They'd voted, and it was like torture getting some of them out on the porch for some fresh air a few minutes each day.

"It's good for your lungs," Nurse Vicky tried telling them.

"My lungs' is just fine," Miguel said. "I stick my head in freezer and breathe."

"Oh, so that's why the meat keeps thawing."

Miguel laughed. "Nurse Vicky, why you never marry?"

"Because men don't listen. Out the door." She gave him a nudge. "Five minutes. Breathe. Go on, all of you."

Jeannie craved the fresh air and liked to go out several times throughout the day, if only for a few minutes each time. It took her longer to put her coat on and blanket spread across her lap and all tucked in, and then to get her hat and scarf on than the actual time she spent outside. But she loved the anticipation and always bundled up eagerly. Nurse Vicky and Lucy loved how she would light up as she gazed out at the farm and the horses and the yurt. "If I have another lifetime, I want to live in a yurt."

"Why you like so much?" Miguel asked.

"I don't know. I guess it's like a big hug, you know, the way it wraps all around you." Jeannie smiled. "And small. I loved those years I lived in a tack room. Small, and yet so cozy. I loved being close to the horses."

Though Vicky had not been a horse person prior to her taking the position of nurse practitioner and caretaker of the old-timers at T-Bone's Place, she couldn't even imagine not being around horses now.

"Did you feel that?"

"What?" Clint asked.

"The change in the wind." As Jeannie looked around, some of the others felt it too. "It's coming," she said. "The storm's coming."

"But it's not supposed to be here for days."

"I know."

"Then how you figure...?" Miguel asked.

Jeannie turned her face to the wind and drew in a deep breath. "This is just the beginning. Mark my words; it's not going to be good."

"Come on," Vicky said. "Let's get you all back inside."

Jeannie was the last to come in. The yearlings were running circles in the pasture, kicking up their heels and having such fun; she wished she could have watched them forever. She glanced back over her shoulder one more time. "Oh, to be that young again."

~ * ~

Top of the list for Liz and Glenda was stocking up on food for the storm; bread, milk, snacks, gallon bottles of spring water, extra toiletries. Apparently, most everyone in town was paying heed to the storm-warnings as well. The grocery store was packed and all the check-out lines were halfway down the food aisles.

Lucy had done the regular shopping for T-Bone's Place earlier in the week, so they were only in need of a few extras. Nurse Vicky had given them a list and they joked about "checking it twice" and "who's naughty and nice" They had two full buggies.

For their part, George and Señor had stacked extra firewood on Ben's porch, and Tom, Dawn, and Junior were stacking extra bales of straw in front of each horse's stall in all three barns.

The National Weather Service was predicting the blizzard would last less than twenty-four hours, but cautioned viewers that the days following the storm could be just as deadly. Glen Riddle, the most respected-most reliable local weatherman urged everyone to plan for at least three days of food and water. Likewise, the Regional Department of Transportation spokesperson insisted they were ready for the storm, but urged viewers to be patient. "Main highways will be cleared first. All parking bans will be in effect. Side streets and rural roads may take up to a week to be cleared;

and that is if there is no additional measurable snow in the three or four days following the storm. Private snowplow vehicles will not be allowed on the roads until they are given an all-clear."

Ben phoned Old-Man Jackson. "If this thing hits and it sure does sound like it's going to...."

"Don't worry about me. I'll be fine."

"I know that, generally as a rule, but...."

"Come on, Ben. We've been through storms before."

"Yes, but not like this one. Not according to what they're saying."

"We all know they've been wrong before. This thing could just blow right over and then what's a little snow. We've been getting dumped on our whole lives. Why are they making such a big deal about this one?"

"I don't know. Maybe they have better ways of predicting storms now."

"Yeah, like the one they missed last year out west when all the cattle died."

"I'm glad you mentioned that. That's my point exactly. Had they been warned...?"

"They weren't. So now they're warning us because they're afraid the same thing's going to happen here and sooner or later they'll be out of a job. If the storm doesn't hit, they're going to say everyone should be happy and meanwhile it's like leaving town when a hurricane is on the way, only to go through all that expense and...."

"Fine. I can understand why you feel that way, but that's not why I called."

"All right, so what did you call for?"

"I'm worried about Veronica and Karen. They said they're not leaving their place either. They said they're not going to leave the horses, and if the roads are closed and they end up in trouble and we can't get to them, I was thinking maybe they could come over to your place, and.... We don't have any stalls left here, how many do you have?"

"I assume you mean the ones that aren't falling apart. In that case, two. And I got horses in each one of them. Hell, it would make more sense for me to go over there. How many horses do they have, five, ten?"

"I think they said only seven at the moment, but that's a good idea. Can I let them know?"

Old Man Jackson paused. "Let them know what?"

"That you'll bring your two horses over there and stay with them and make sure everything's okay."

"No. I....I don't think so. That damn Veronica'll drive me nuts and neither one of them can cook. What happens if I get snowed in with them for days? I'm liable to tack up Zeenya and ride off into the sunset looking for a McDonald's that's open."

Ben laughed. "No problem. The women here are planning to take them over food for a week the day before. You'll be just fine."

Jackson's silence implied he was giving the idea some thought. "How will we heat it?"

"They have a wood burner. They heat with wood. They can heat everything up on top of the wood burner. What are you planning to eat if you don't go?"

"Damn, Ben. You're hitting me where it hurts."

## *Three Days Before Christmas*

Linda and Susie spent the afternoon at the Vet Hospital giving the stalls a top-to-bottom thorough scrubbing. It was standard procedure to sterilize a stall after each equine patient was discharged, but since they were essentially closing down for a week it seemed like a good time to do some extra sanitation. Taking advantage of this downtime would also spare Cindy having to smell the heavy-duty disinfectant. She was no longer experiencing morning sickness, but certain odors still upset her stomach, and in Marvin's words, the outcome was not pretty.

As it was, Susie and Linda were both wearing surgical masks and more than once had to leave the general stall area to try to clear their lungs and catch their breath. "You sure you didn't mix that too strong?" Linda asked.

"Positive," Susie said, coughing.

Linda raised the overhead door in the patient receiving area to let some fresh air inside. "Hey, come look at the sky."

Susie coughed her way over next to her. "Wow!" Half of it was bright blue with rays of sunshine and the other half as black as night.

"Wait. Did you just hear that?" Linda asked. "Was that thunder?"

Susie removed her mask as if that would help her listen better.

They heard it again. "That *was* thunder, wasn't it?"

"I don't know. I didn't see any lightning. Did you?"

Linda shook her head. "I've heard of thunder snow, but it's not snowing." Just then, a bolt of lightning sliced down through the darkest part of the sky. "Oh my God, that was amazing!"

13

Susie pointed across the pasture. "Look, it's Hillary."

Linda yelled to her. "Did you see that?"

Hillary waved. "I love it!" The air was so still they could hear one another perfectly through the bare trees in the woods between Hillary and Matthew's yurt and the Vet Hospital. "I got a really awesome picture of it!"

Susie shivered at the sudden change in the air.

"I just checked radar! It's gonna come sooner than they thought."

"When?"

"Mid-day Christmas Eve!"

Another bolt of distant lightning tore through the black sky. "This is too cool!" Linda yelled.

"What?"

"I said, it's too cool!!"

The wind had apparently shifted.

"Take off your mask," Susie said.

Linda dropped her mask down, the way a jockey would their goggles. "I said this is too cool!"

"I know!" Hillary yelled back. "I can't stand it!"

"Me neither!"

"I'm shutting the door now," Susie said.

"See you at dinner!" Linda yelled, stooping down lower and lower as the door closed further and further.

"I'm feeling the earth energy, are you?"

"Oh yeah!"

~ * ~

Ben went a day early to his regular barber shop for a haircut and since it was so close to Nottingham Downs, from habit he found himself turning right instead of left out of the parking lot and was on his way to the racetrack. If it weren't

14

for Hillary and all her talk of destiny and fate and how everything happens for a reason, he might have laughed off his absentminded mistake and turned around, but for that very reason he kept right on going. He wasn't a fan of the casino in any way shape or form, which was open twenty-four-seven all year, and also as was his habit he drove past the club entrance and pulled into the stable gate.

He hadn't really expected there to be security at the guard shack, and yet, as he pulled up to the locked gate and sat there looking in at what for all practical purposes should have been an abandoned barn area, a woman in uniform approached his truck, her hand on her hip covering what appeared to be a revolver.

She motioned for Ben to put down his window.

Ben obliged. "What are you doing here?"

"No. The question should be more like, what are *you* doing here?"

"I'm not rightly sure," Ben said.

"Say what?"

Ben smiled to ease her concern. "I was just driving down the road, and...."

"The track is closed, sir. There's no racing going on."

"Then why are you here?"

"I work here. It's my job to be here. Now you....uh...."

"I'm Ben Miller." He extended his hand. "I'm the owner of this racetrack."

The woman laughed. "Yeah, and I'm the winner of last week's lottery. I'm just finishing out my shift till they send the limo."

Ben chuckled and in an effort to legitimize himself opened his glove compartment to look for his horsemen's license.

"Sir?" The woman stepped back, her hand on her revolver.

"Oh. Don't worry," Ben said. "I'm just getting my license. I just got a haircut and I'm not really sure why I decided to come on ahead to the track. Oh, here it is. Here." Ben handed her his Owner-Trainer License. "See. That's me."

The woman studied the photo. "Okay, you're an owner, trainer, and you just got a haircut. They did a nice job, by the way. If you'll just stay put, I need to call somebody."

Ben nodded. "They're all on Holiday."

The guard glanced at the jam-packed casino parking lot. "My supervisor is here, so...."

Ben smiled. "How about I just leave?"

"Uh, how about you just stay put." The guard glanced at his license plate.

Ben shrugged. "Whatever. I'm serious, I...."

The woman walked away and went inside the guard shack to make her phone call. Meanwhile, Ben sat looking at the barn area; so deserted, so desolate. That's when he heard the thunder. He turned the radio down, thinking he must've left it on.

"Mr. Miller."

Ben looked at the woman. He hadn't realized she'd returned.

"I'm sorry. I uh...." She handed him his license. "Please don't fire me."

"What? For doing your job? Did you just hear thunder?"

"Yes," she said, warily. "I thought I did. I thought it might have been...."

Ben put his license away. "Can you let me in now?"

"Yes sir."

When she unlocked the gate and stepped aside, Ben drove on through and as he glanced in his rearview mirror, he noted how she locked the gate behind him. "I hope her shift doesn't end soon," he said to himself. That's when he heard the rumble of distant thunder again. He glanced up at the clouds, so dark, but yet so far away.

As he drove slowly around the backside area, a stern wind blew a hay string across the path in front of him. It reminded him of tumbleweed and he started singing, "Tumble wee-ee-ee-eed...." He imagined ghosts haunting the place and in his mind's eye, he could see horses going back and forth to the racetrack. He tried only imagining the good times, but the bad times kept creeping in. He parked his truck by the track kitchen, got out and walked up to the racetrack and again out of habit, he stood in his favorite place on the rail.

"Meg, are you there?"

"Yes," he could hear her soft voice say.

"What are you doing here?"

"I don't know. I guess I just wanted to visit for a while today. There's a winter storm coming."

"I know." Ben smiled, his eyes tearing from the wind. Or was it from.... "I miss you, Meg."

"I miss you too."

"I just...." Ben swiped at a tear trickling down his cheek.

"Now, now...don't be sad. Be happy so I can be happy, because when you're sad, I'm sad."

"I'll try," Ben said.

It was then that a bolt of lightning lit up the sky and with the flash, the numbers on the infield tote board blinked again and again.

"All right, all right," Ben said, with a hardy laugh. "I get it! I'll be happy!"

"Good. Let's go home now."

~ * ~

Dinner at Meg's Meadows was as lively as usual with at least five different conversations going on simultaneously. "They're saying the storm, depending on the wind, could possibly arrive way sooner than anticipated. It's all dependent on the wind," Señor declared.

"Isn't that the case with all weather?" George asked.

Señor laughed. "You know, I've had just about enough of you for one day."

"What? I was just asking?"

"I made three batches of brownies today," Marvin said. "I didn't want to make them early, but with the wind picking up and all...."

Señor smiled. "Okay, so maybe I'm a little obsessed with the weather."

"A little?" several of them echoed.

Liz changed the subject slightly. "Is the plan still to smoke the turkeys?"

"Yes. Why not?" Señor asked.

"I don't know. With the wind...."

Señor shook his head. "That was a cheap shot."

"No, actually I'm serious. Will it affect the draft you need on the smoker?"

"You mean, like the wind?" Randy asked.

Señor just looked at him.

"Come on, Dad. Get with it."

"You know what else?" D.R. said from in the living room. "It's going to be a wet snow and very good for making a snowman. Only maybe not. You know why?"

Everyone looked at him. "No, why, son?"

D.R. paused for effect. "It'll depend on the wind."

Everyone laughed, even Maeve and Maria, who had no idea what was so funny.

"Actually," Dawn said. "Depending on the wind, I heard the latest prediction is up to two feet of snow, maybe more."

Ben sat back and looked around at everyone. "Are we prepared?"

They all turned to Señor for an answer. "Yes," he said. "As prepared as we're ever going to be. All kidding aside, wind or no wind, I think we've got everything covered."

## *Two Days Before Christmas*

It was an extremely odd weather day. The sky was still black and blue, but the wind was practically non-existent. Even though there was very little snow on the ground the children tried making a snowman and ultimately gave up.

"I'm cold."

"Me too."

"Me too."

Dawn took them back inside and spent the afternoon making additional batches of brownies and pumpkin pies with Liz. All the casseroles had already been made, cooled, and then frozen. All the Christmas cookies had already been made. Some of those too were already frozen. The plan was for all of the holiday side dishes to be made early tomorrow in case the power went out during the night Christmas Eve when the heaviest snowfall was expected.

Liz glanced at her daughter-in-law from across the kitchen counter. "For someone who says they can't bake, you sure are doing a wonderful job."

Dawn smiled. "You taught me."

"Did your mother like to bake?"

Dawn shook her head. "No. She actually didn't cook much at all. We always had a chef."

"What about your Aunt Maeve?"

Dawn chuckled. "She was a snack freak. Always munching on goodies. If she were here, she would have eaten half the brownies by now. She insisted healthy eating was highly overrated." Liz watched Dawn's expression change as she relived the briefest of fond memories, and ultimately the sadness. "I miss them."

Liz nodded. "I know. Sadness has a way of visiting often, even when you think it's far, far away. It's never so far that it can't come knocking on your door."

Dawn looked at her.

"Our choice is do we invite the sadness in for a while or do we just acknowledge its presence and respectfully close the door."

~ * ~

All six dogs; five Labrador Retrievers and a Standard Poodle, observed the flurry of activity without the least concern. Each day leading up to Christmas probably seemed like any other day to them. They romped and played outside, took lots of naps in the barn or on any number of porches at Meg's Meadows or in any one of the kitchens. And at the end of the day, they followed Dusty upstairs to his loft apartment in the broodmare barn to bed down for the night.

They had a routine, the horses had a routine, the residents had a routine. It wasn't until late in the day that there was any inkling the animals knew or suspected a winter storm was on the horizon. Maybe they all started sensing an urgency in the way their caretakers were going about their business. Maybe there was something in their manner or a change in their voices. Perhaps the signal came by way of a drop in barometric pressure. By late afternoon, the horses were all a little more restless, a little more anxious to come inside. But by far, it was the dogs that seemed to be heeding the call of the wild and sounding the alarm. They barked at each and every wind gust and when the wind would calm down, they barked in apparent anticipation of when it would flare up again. Surprisingly, the dog with the loudest, roughest, toughest bark was Rotty, the Standard Poodle and he always had plenty to say. He was sounding the alarm.

~ * ~

Señor made a trip to the lumber yard to pick up snowplow markers for the walking path and spent the afternoon pounding them all in place. This was the first winter for the new path that essentially circled all of Meg's Meadows. A lot of hard work had gone into its construction and he didn't want the Gator and snowplow tearing it up in any way, shape, or form. Cracker Jack Henderson came out onto the back porch at T-Bone's Place to chat a minute.

"So, do you think it's going to be as bad as they say?"

Señor nodded. "From all indications, yes, and then some."

Cracker Jack's wild and crazy long white hair billowed around his head in the wind. "I rode out a hurricane once, lived to tell the tale, and vowed I'd never do it again."

Señor glanced at him as he lined up another marker.

"My son offered to get me a flight to his place in South Carolina, but I said no, I can't leave my friends here. I told him they're my family too. Besides, they might need me and he doesn't."

Señor nodded, pounding on the stake.

"You're blessed to have your son and daughter and grandchildren here with you."

Señor agreed.

"Do you have other children?"

"No, we lost one."

"I'm sorry to hear that."

"Yeah, it was rough. Randy and Cindy were so young and Liz being so sick...." Señor wiped his brow and just stared for a moment. "We almost lost her too. Thank God she pulled through. Otherwise, who knows how the kids would have turned out or where I'd be."

Cracker Jack smiled. "You have a fine family, Señor, and by the grace of God, so do I. Here, and in South Carolina. We have a lot to be thankful for. Now if only this storm would just pass us by...."

~ * ~

Wendy spent the afternoon cleaning the bathrooms and then tidied up the kitchen and living room. If the storm prediction materialized, there would be sixteen adults and five children staying overnight at Ben's farmhouse on Christmas Eve. That was sixteen including her son Gordon if it didn't start snowing too soon in Buffalo and Erie which was on his way. Both areas were under the same blizzard warning.

"Can you leave earlier?" she'd asked him on the phone.

"No, I have a client meeting Saturday morning."

"But...."

"Don't worry, Mom. I'll be there, eventually."

She wished he hadn't added *eventually*. She wished he didn't live so far away. As she stared out the kitchen window at the gently falling snow, she recalled Christmases when he and Matthew were little boys and how they'd run down the stairs in their pajamas Christmas morning, their hair all tousled and their little bare feet. Such wonderful memories to cherish. She also remembered their first Christmas without their father. They were both so young when he passed away. He was such a good man, a good father and a good husband. She mourned his death for years and raised her sons by herself, wishing....

Then she met Tom, the exact opposite of her first husband in so many ways; both good men, kind and loving, one a businessman and one a cowboy. Both the man of her dreams. She smiled as she watched Tom leading the ponies into the barn. He was like the Pied Piper. They'd follow him anywhere. Even Sadie, the little blind Shetland Pony. She was right on his heels.

When the phone rang, she turned, staring at it as if it were a ghost. The landline hardly ever rang. They all used their cellphones. Why was it ringing? Who on earth could be calling? She walked over and picked it up. "Hello."

It was a recording. "This is a weather alert. Extreme weather conditions are forecast for the next twenty-four to thirty-six hours. Lake Effect areas can expect up to three feet of heavy snow. Attempting to use your ovens for heat in the event of a power failure is extremely dangerous. For medical assistance, please contact your local fire department. We advise you have emergency numbers listed near your phone. We repeat. This is a weather alert."

~ * ~

Ben stopped by to check on the old-timers, his regular routine at least once or twice a week and assured them everything was being done to keep them safe and sound and to not worry. Each of them had a worst-storm-story they'd lived through and not surprisingly most were when they were inside a barn or elsewhere on the backside of a racetrack.

"The hail hit the dorms so hard it broke all the windows in the building. I hid under my cot."

"I was in the track kitchen. Several of us ran up there last minute. We figured it was the safest place being made of cement block. Not only that, we knew there'd be food there. I'd never seen a storm like that in my life."

"I was in the feed room. Even the mice were scared. They were running everywhere."

"Me, I made it to my truck and no sooner had I gotten inside and shut the door, here it came. It rocked the truck something fierce. I thought it was going to blow us over on our side."

"For me, the worst storm was when we were warming up for a race. This was back before everyone went with ponies. It started raining so hard you couldn't see the horses in front of you. People were yelling, Over here! Over here! Someone had opened the gate by the gap and out we all went into the first barn we could find. We were there for hours till it let up enough for the grooms to come get their horses."

"Aren't you supposed to go back to the paddock under those circumstances?"

"In that lightning? Ain't no way."

"We actually all got fined, but they eventually had to waive all of them. We refused to ride when the ruling came down. They thought we were kidding and we weren't. Back then we stuck together."

They all nodded. Then everyone looked at Jeannie for some reason. "Mark my words," she said. "This is going to be a bad storm."

For once, no one argued with her.

"I can feel it in my bones."

~ * ~

With the latest weather update predicting even more snow than originally anticipated, Señor decided he needed to shore up the back porch at T-Bone's Place. He didn't like the pitch; a rather flat angle for the roof, and feared three feet of wet snow might be too much for it to support.

Nurse Vicky seemed rather alarmed.

"Better this than have it cave in," Señor said.

"What? Do you think it will?"

"No. That's why I'm putting this brace in. I want to make sure it *doesn't* happen."

"Has it ever happened before?"

"I don't know. I doubt it. Otherwise the roof angle would've been changed by now."

Nurse Vicky sighed. "What should I tell the residents?"

Señor just looked at her for a moment. "Tell them the truth; that is a precaution and better safe than sorry."

Nurse Vicky nodded. "Maybe I'll leave off the sorry part."

Señor smiled. Judging just from her reaction.... "Maybe that's a good idea."

Lucy came out onto the porch to see what was going on. "Wait a minute, aren't our bedrooms over the porch?"

"No," Señor said. "They're over the main part of the house."

"You sure? Not even part of it?"

Señor just looked at her.

"Sorry. I just...."

"I understand. No problem. By the way, George'll be back with the Christmas trees soon. Dawn and the kids went with him. A table topper for here and a big one for Ben's. We all decided not to have one for each house as we don't know when we'll be back in them."

Lucy wrapped her arms to fend off the cold. "Do you think it's going to be bad?"

"That all depends on how you look at it. One thing for sure, it's probably going to be a Christmas none of us will likely ever forget."

~ * ~

By the time everyone gathered at Dawn and Randy's for dinner, snow flurries were just starting to intensify and accumulate. The actual blizzard wasn't supposed to hit until mid-morning to mid-day tomorrow on Christmas Eve *depending on the wind.*

"Oh no, not the wind again."

Señor laughed. "Did you know there is a phone app that updates you on your local weather every half hour regardless if there has been a change."

"What do they say?" Matthew asked. "Same-o, same-o."

"No, they give you a full report, but I'm finding they change the wording slightly."

"Probably so they don't bore the average normal person."

Señor laughed. "What? Are you saying I'm not average or normal?"

"No, I'm just saying the average person probably wouldn't notice it's the same report worded differently or even care."

"I resemble that."

"Pass me the butter, please."

"I went to the racetrack today," Ben said.

Dawn looked at him. "You did? Why?"

"I don't know for sure, but did you know the stable gate has guards on duty throughout the winter?"

"No."

They all looked at Wendy. "That's news to me," she said. "I wonder why."

"That's what I was wondering. Who would know?"

"Richard probably, but he and Heather are still on vacation in the Bahamas."

"Where it's warm," Tom added with emphasis.

Wendy looked at him.

"Hey, there's times I miss Florida in the winter. That's all."

"Really?" Wendy saddened at the thought. She loved winter.

"I said sometimes, not all the time, not now, maybe tomorrow."

Wendy smiled.

"So, what's the track look like? I've never been there in the winter."

"It looks like a ghost town," Ben said.

"Real ghosts, Grandpa?" D. R. asked.

"Well, as real as a ghost can be, I guess."

"I like ghosts," Maeve said.

"Me too," Maria echoed.

Randy smiled. "Do you think the day's going to come when those two disagree with one another?"

"I hope not," Linda said. "I want them to be friends for life."

"You don't have to agree all the time to be friends," Randy said.

Linda looked at him. "Shut up."

Everyone laughed.

"Oh boy," Señor said, glancing at his cellphone. "They just upped the ante."

"What do you mean?" Liz asked.

"They're calling this the One Hundred Year Winter Storm."

Marvin looked at him. "Is that just a change of wording, or...?"

"Nope. This time tomorrow afternoon, we could possibly have three feet of snow or more."

Tears welled up in Wendy's eyes.

"What's wrong?" Tom asked.

"Gordon will never be able to make it. I should tell him not to even try."

"Mom, come on," Matthew said. "He's got all-wheel drive."

"And a BMW no less," Tom said.

Wendy shook her head, tears spilling down her cheeks. "But it's too low to the ground. You've seen it. He's never going to make it. He wouldn't even make it if it had a snowplow on the front of it. He's just too low to the ground."

Tom looked at her for a moment, feeling helpless to do or say much of anything to comfort her. But then he had a thought and took out his cellphone. "Gordon, rent a Jeep," he texted, and got an immediate reply.

"I'll try."

Tom texted back. "That or a tank. It's the only way you're going to get through."

# *Christmas Eve*

There was five inches of new snow on the ground by morning and a lot to be done before the worst of the storm was due to hit. With a temporary lull in the amount of snow falling at the moment, the horses were turned out in their pastures to romp and play. They loved the snow; they loved to roll in it, loved to run in it, love to paw in it, and loved to fill their mouths with it. There was beauty in their not knowing they would probably be stuck in their stalls for the next few days or possibly longer. For the moment, it was all fun and frolic. They had ice crystals on their nose hairs and snowflakes on their eyelashes.

Señor had slow-smoked a turkey overnight to take to Karen and Veronica at Shifting Gears and by the time the pop-up thermometer indicated it was done, he had all the side dishes along with the rest of their meals for the week loaded up in his truck. Ben rode over with him and Old Man Jackson met them there with his two horses in his trailer. The filly Zeenya was all full of herself and almost got away from him as soon as he unloaded her. "Tell the wind to stop blowing till I get her in the barn," Jackson said, laughing and yet holding on to her for dear life. "Thatta girl. Thatta girl.... Whoa now, thatta girl." His older horse walked off calm as can be and eyed the barn right from the start.

When both horses were settled in, they all made several trips back and forth from Señor's truck to Karen and Veronica's kitchen with all the food, plus jugs of water and milk.

"I'm lactose intolerant," Veronica said, wringing her hands as she watched Señor put the milk in the fridge.

"Then I suggest you not drink it," Old Man Jackson said. "All the more for me that way anyway."

Ben glanced at him. "Now, you know, you're all going to have to behave."

"Behave?"

As Karen handed Señor another carton of milk Ben noticed a list of items taped to the kitchen cabinet. "Hogwash?" It was only one checked off. "What's with the hogwash?"

"It's hooch. At least that's what *we* call it."

Old Man Jackson laughed. "Hot damn!"

"It's just in case."

"Just in case of what?"

"In case we feel the need to have some."

~ * ~

Next stop was to fill up the extra gas cans. Their storage tank at the farm had been topped off two weeks ago and understandably the gas company was not allowing any additional deliveries because of the blizzard warning for fear of running out.

"Happy to see they're not price gouging," Señor said. "Can't imagine people doing that, and yet...."

Ben nodded. "The inhumanity of humanity."

"Wow, Ben. That's heavy."

"I know." Ben laughed. "Wonder where that came from?"

There was a line of at least five or six vehicles at every pump. When it was their turn, Señor climbed into the bed of his pickup and after Ben filled each gas can, he would slide it to the other side and hand him another.

Ben yelled to a man two bays away. "Hey, Jocko! You doing good?"

"Yeah, we're all ready. You too?"

"Yep. Merry Christmas!"

The man waved and pulled out, his tires slipping and sliding in the ever-increasing snow. When Ben went inside to pay, he glanced at the rack of candy next to the counter. "Give me two of those bags of licorice for good luck," he said to the cashier.

The woman rang up the purchase. "I think we're going to need it. The good luck that is."

Ben smiled reassuringly. "Make that three bags of licorice then and I'll leave one for you."

~ * ~

Most everyone at Meg's Meadows was home by mid-afternoon Christmas Eve. All but Randy, Mark, and Wendy's son Gordon, who she had yet to hear from today. She hoped he was well on his way home from New York by now, but also hoped if the roads were as dangerous as the news channels were reporting, that he had changed his mind about trying to make it, and....

The phone rang.

She picked up the receiver quickly, hoping it was Gordon without giving thought to how he had never called the landline before. It was another weather alert. She stared out the window at the falling snow while listening to the gloom and doom, her heart heavy with fear and trepidation. Then up the front steps came Tom and George with the Christmas tree and she couldn't help but smile. The tree was taller than both of them and rather awkward to handle, but the funny part was when they used the leaf blower to rid it of snow before they brought it inside, both spitting and sputtering as they blew snow all over one another. They looked like little boys, two silly little boys just having fun, and then once again she saddened.

"Come see our snowman," she could hear Matthew as a child saying.

"Hurry, Mom. Hurry!" In her mind's eye she could see Gordon waving from outside the window. "Hurry!"

Tom glanced at her as they brought the tree inside the front doorway backwards. "Did you hear from Gordon?"

He figured that was why she was smiling. "No, not today yet. I was just remembering...."

"Okay, where do you want it?" George asked.

Wendy laughed. Their Christmas tree always went in the same place every year in front of the living room window. Yet he always asked. "Right there," she said.

They already had it attached to the stand. It just needed to be filled with water. George stood back to admire the seven-foot blue spruce. "This may be our best one yet." He always said that too.

"I agree." Tom said. And so did she. "Where's Ben?"

"He walked over to T-Bone's."

"In that?" Tom pointed out the window.

"We were just there," George said. "I didn't see him."

"He left a few minutes ago."

All three walked to the kitchen window and looked out. They could see the path from here to T-Bone's even with it snowing. No Ben. "Should we call him?" Wendy asked.

Tom shook his head. "I'm not calling him. I don't want him thinking I'm watch-dogging him."

"Where *are* the dogs anyway?" George asked.

"They're with Dusty," Wendy said.

Tom looked out the window again. "George, why don't you call him."

"Oh no. Not me. I ain't going down that road."

"Wait. Listen...." Wendy said. "Do you hear that?"

"What?"

"Listen...."

It was Ben, coming up the driveway and singing as he walked along. "We wish you a Merry Christmas. We wish you a Merry Christmas. We wish you a Merrrrrryyyyy Christmas and a Happy New Year."

~ * ~

When it came time to bring all the horses in, again it was all-hands on deck. Between George, Glenda, Tom, Dawn, and Randy they were all back in the barn, wiped off, and snug in their stalls in less than an hour's time.

"I love that sound," Dawn said.

"The wind, you mean?" Randy asked.

"No, the horses munching their hay."

"I knew that." Randy wrapped his arms around her.

"It's so peaceful. I feel like I'm in an igloo."

"The snow's insulating the barn."

"I'll come back and grain just before dinner," George said, sliding the main barn door open. "Oh, wow. It's really coming down now."

"I'd say it's finally here," Tom said.

Along with the heavier snowfall the wind gusts had picked up significantly and could be seen swirling across the paddocks. Señor was making his third pass around the walking path with the Gator plow and D.R. was sitting at his side with one hand on the wheel. When everyone leaving the barn waved to him, he had a big grin on his face. He was all bundled up, warm as can be in the enclosed cab.

Randy smiled. His little man on the job. It reminded him of days gone by when he was working side-by-side with his dad. "He's like the energizer bunny," George said. "He never tires."

Randy nodded. "He's tough as nails. He always has been. I dread the day he starts to slow down. It won't sit well with him. He'll drive us all nuts," he added, to make light of the thought of his father slowing down in any way, shape, or form.

Tom took out his phone and glanced at a text message.

"Everything okay?" Dawn asked.

"No." Tom quickly put his phone back in his pocket to keep it from getting wet from the snow. "Gordon just hit a roadblock, literally. He's stuck in a gridlock."

"Where?"

"Just this side of Rochester."

"Oh Jesus."

Tom nodded. "My sentiments exactly. Ain't no way he's going to make it but I'll wait to hear from him for sure before I tell Wendy."

~ * ~

After begging and begging, just before dinner and with the Lake Effect snow machine on full blast, Maeve, Maria, Julie, Ashley, and D.R. were allowed outside to play in the snow, but only for a little while. The dogs frolicked with them, scooting along on their sides and their backs, rolling and rolling and making all sorts of snow angels alongside the children's. Their paw prints and images disappeared within minutes amidst the giggling and barking and howling.

35

When it was time for them to go back inside, the dogs raced them to the side door and Marvin helped Ashley up the steps. She was so bundled up she looked like a little penguin, arms out to her sides and waddling. "Oh my, you weigh a ton."

Those that hadn't gathered at Ben's house yet, soon all came straggling in, looking like abominable snowmen. Extra rugs had been put down just inside the door and took on most of the snow, which soon melted, and more rugs were then put down. The dogs were relegated to the utility room until they were dried off with towel after towel.

"You'd swear they were out in the rain," Dusty said, fluffing Rotty's hair. The only poodle in the pack of Labradors, she was the wettest of them all.

Señor put more logs on the fire. "Any word from Gordon?"

"No," Wendy shook her head. "I've tried calling him several times but there's never any answer."

Señor had been watching the weather channel. It was not looking promising for Gordon's direct route home and taking backroads wasn't advised as they would likely be worse. "Did I hear someone say he rented a Jeep?"

"No," he tried. "There were none available."

"Dinner's ready," Liz said.

The children squealed and ran to their table and chairs, not that they were all that hungry. They'd been told countless times all week whenever they asked, that they'd be decorating the Christmas tree *after dinner* on Christmas Eve and that before they went to bed, they'd each be able to open one gift. Plus, they had been practicing a song about the Baby Jesus and tomorrow was the day they would finally get to sing it.

"Remember, it's a surprise," Carol said. "No telling."

"You hear that?" D. R. said to the others. "No telling."

"You're the tattletale," Maeve said. "You tell everything."

"No, I don't."

"Yes, you do," Maria said.

Julie and Ashley agreed, though Ashley's agreeing didn't carry all that much leverage. She was just learning to talk and had no idea what a tattletale was. "Yes, you do too."

"Yeah, well, I'm not telling this."

~ * ~

Christmas Eve dinner was a family favorite; Meg's lasagna, tossed salad, garlic bread, Grandma's Gelatin Salad, and for dessert, Cassata Cake. As usual, there were numerous conversations going on at the same time.

"The old-timers decorated their tree this afternoon and they've already eaten their dinner. "Most of them are in their pajamas already," Lucy said.

"I heard from Veronica a little while ago. She and Karen and Old Man Jackson are getting along so far."

That brought a chuckle from everyone.

"I guess he tied a rope from their back door of their house to the barn just in case they needed to find their way. Veronica was worried they wouldn't be able to see the barn in the blizzard and Jackson got tired of hearing her fret."

Tom passed his plate to Wendy. "Another helping of lasagna, please."

"By the way, I heard from Richard," she said. "He has no idea why there is a guard at the stable gate. He's going to check when he and Heather get home. He said to wish everyone a Merry Christmas. Oh, and it's eighty-five degrees there."

"Bah Humbug," Dusty said.

They all laughed.

"It's a Christmas Carol," Maeve said.

Randy turned. "What?"

"Bah Humbug. It the Christmas Carol."

"We're going to sing a Christmas Carol."

"No, we're not," D.R. said, frowning at her in the most critical way.

Maeve just looked at him. "I didn't say anything."

Randy laughed. "Eat. Both of you."

"Are the horses all done for the night?" Ben asked.

George nodded. "We'll check on them before we go over to T-Bone's."

Mark dished himself a third helping of lasagna. "I got dibs on Frank's recliner."

"Not if I get to it first," George said.

"Which reminds me." Glenda took a sip of water. "I heard from Skip down the road earlier. He wanted to know if we were worried about the storm. I said, have you looked outside?"

Instinctively, everyone looked out the window.

"If this keeps up...." Junior said.

"It's got to be over a foot already since noon."

"Try sixteen inches," Señor said, glancing at his cellphone.

"How much in Rochester and Buffalo?" Wendy asked.

Señor punched in the locations. "Close to two feet."

"What about Erie?"

"A little more,"

Wendy looked at Tom, sadness written all over her face. It was then that Rotty got up and walked over and put his head in her lap, wagging his tail. "You know you're not allowed to beg," she said, with tears welling up in her eyes.

Hillary smiled. "I don't think he's begging. I think he's trying to make you feel better."

Wendy gazed deep into the dog's eyes and patted him gently. "Thank you, Rotty. I needed that. I really did. Thank you...."

~ * ~

"I should have brought my rocking chair," Old Man Jackson said, trying to get comfortable on the rickety couch at Shifting Gears.

"It's not too late," Karen teased. "Maybe you can get stuck in the snow somewhere."

Jackson laughed.

"That's nothing to kid about," Veronica said. "He could seriously get stuck somewhere."

Karen rolled her eyes. "I was kidding. All right? Lighten up."

"Yeah, well what if I was kidding too? Maybe you should be the one to lighten up."

Jackson glanced from one to the other. "You two are downright amazing. You know that?"

Karen smiled. "Was that a compliment?"

"No." Jackson laughed. "Not in the least."

"Aw, come on. Say something nice. It's Christmas Eve."

"All right." Jackson thought for a moment and for effect stroked his chin as if he really had to think long and hard. "Let me see I'm sure there's something I could praise about you two."

"I didn't say praise, I just said something nice."

Jackson smiled. "Well, in that case, that's easy. You both *are* amazing."

39

Karen and Veronica just looked at him.

"I'm serious. I admire you two. You're both a little strange, but I have nothing but admiration for both of you. What you do for horses, it's been your life's work. And you ask nothing in return from anyone, just that the horses get well and get taken care of, and even when...." Jackson paused and shook his head in wonder. "I'll tell you what, I couldn't do it. It takes a special kind of person to do what you two do. If there is a heaven you two are going to be up there in first class."

Veronica swallowed hard and wiped her eyes. Karen just smiled.

"Now that's it. No more nice-nice."

Karen laughed. "Wait a minute. What do you mean *if* there's a heaven?"

"Well, I'll tell you what, if I get there ahead of you, I'll make sure to come back and let you know."

"Don't you be haunting us," Veronica said.

Jackson smiled. "I wouldn't dream of it. It'll be a friendly visit, that I can tell you for sure."

~ * ~

No sooner had Gordon gotten through one roadblock, he came upon another. The patrolman directing traffic motioned for him to roll down his window. "How far are you going?"

"Ohio."

The patrolman shook his head. "Good luck."

Gordon looked up at the man. "Meaning...?"

"Meaning, unless Santa Claus swoops his reindeer down here to take you for a sleighride, it ain't happening.

40

Sorry. Local traffic only. I'm going to have to ask you to turn around."

"But where will I go? Is there another route I can take?"

"I can't tell you what's even open at this point." Falling snow collected on the officer's hat, his face red from the cold. "There's an old truck route. You can try that. It's back about a mile."

Gordon stared ahead at what looked like Alaska tundra. "My mom is expecting me for Christmas. This will be my first Christmas that I'm not home."

"I'm sorry, son." The officer glanced over his shoulder at the row of headlights behind them. "It's not going to let up. This is only the beginning. If you take that route, tuck yourself in behind a semi. It'll be your only chance."

Gordon nodded.

"Gas up and make sure you have plenty of water and something to eat along the way. There's a station at the intersection. Turn right."

"Thank you."

"Good luck, son."

~ * ~

The task of stringing the lights on the Meg's Meadows Christmas tree had become an annual tradition for Tom and he took the responsibility quite seriously. The lights had to be placed just so, no dark areas whatsoever and they had to go the whole way around. He'd been known to take them all off and start over again if they weren't just right.

The children waited anxiously for their part. "Come on already," D.R. said.

"Now-now, you can't rush a masterpiece."

41

"Why don't you just start in the middle," Maria said.

"The middle?"

"Put it around the middle and then go up with one end...." She raised her arm. "And down with the other."

Maeve agreed with the idea. "That way you can see what you have left."

Tom smiled. "Wow, for little pipsqueaks you two sure do know your stuff. Now D.R. on the other hand...."

D.R. slumped his adolescent shoulders in utter exasperation. "Uncle Tom. The lights, okay?"

"Fine." When all the lights were hung, everyone had a say as to what would come next. "Garland?"

"Yes."

"Silver and gold? Or red and green?"

"Red and green."

"Icicles?"

"No. Remember last year."

"Good point." There were icicles everywhere.

"Color ornaments or silver and gold?" Wendy opened both boxes.

"Color," yelled the children, each reaching in to grab one.

"I'm sensing a pattern here. Uh, same thing last year too."

Every last color ornament was hung on the tree, the bottom heavy-laden since that's obviously where the children could reach best, unless an adult picked them up so they could reach higher. Ben sat in his easy chair, sipping coffee and marveling. Meg would love this. The children all scurrying about, grabbing ornaments as fast as they could, placing them everywhere and anywhere. The laughter, the teasing, and everyone getting in one another's way. The colors of the ornaments all seemed to be congregated in

42

certain areas too, depending on Maeve, Maria, Julie, and Ashley's preferences.

"It's perfect," Ben said. "It's absolutely beautiful."

Everyone agreed, the children squealing with delight. "Do we get to open our one present now?" Julie asked.

"Yes." Liz pretended to search each pile for just the right ones, and not so coincidently they all got a pair of new pajamas that were specific with the patterns of cartoon characters they each loved.

"Imagine that," Dusty said.

"All right, everybody," Carol said, herding the children. "Let's go get ready for bed."

"Can we wear our new pajamas?" Maria asked.

"Of course. It's Christmas Eve."

When the children had all left the room, for the first time of many times that evening, the power blipped.

"Oh no!" Julie yelled. "The lights are stopping."

"It's okay. They're back on."

"They're doing it again," D.R. said.

Señor yawned as he put a couple more logs on the fire. "It's going to be a long night."

"A long winter's night," several of them echoed.

D.R. stuck his head out into the hallway from one of the bedrooms. "How will you read the Christmas story in the dark if the lights keep blinking, Grandpa?"

"Don't you worry," Ben said. "I have a flashlight."

When the children had all returned to the living room and gathered on blankets on the floor in front of Ben, the dogs edged their way in between and around them. Photos were being taken from just about every adult in the room, and then they all settled back to hear Ben read the children a Christmas story.

There was magic in their eyes, magic in the room. The lights didn't blink once while Ben read the story. And though the wind howled outside, they were all warm and snug, a fire crackling in the fireplace and a Christmas tree of all Christmas trees shining bright.

'Twas the night before Christmas, when all through the house
Not a creature was stirring, not even a mouse.
The stockings were hung by the chimney with care,
In hopes that St. Nicholas soon would be there;
The children were nestled all snug in their beds,
While visions of sugar-plums danced in their heads;
And mamma in her 'kerchief, and I in my cap,
Had just settled down for a long winter's nap,

When out on the lawn there arose such a clatter,
I sprang from the bed to see what was the matter.
Away to the window I flew like a flash,
Tore open the shutters and threw up the sash.
The moon on the breast of the new-fallen snow
Gave the luster of mid-day to objects below,
When, what to my wondering eyes should appear,
But a miniature sleigh, and eight tiny reindeer,

With a little old driver, so lively and quick,
I knew in a moment it must be St. Nick.
More rapid than eagles his coursers they came.
And he whistled and shouted and called them by name;
"Now, Dasher!  Now, Dancer! Now, Prancer, and Vixen!
On, Comet! On Cupid! On, Donner and Blitzen!
To the top of the porch! To the top of the wall!
Now dash away, dash away, dash away all!"

As dry leaves that before the wild hurricane fly,
When they meet with an obstacle, mount to the sky,
So up to the house-top the coursers they flew,
With the sleigh full of toys, and St. Nicholas too.
And then, in a twinkling, I heard on the roof
The prancing and pawing of each little hoof.
As I drew in my hand, and was turning around,
Down the chimney St. Nicholas came with a bound.

He was dressed all in fur, from his head to his foot,
And his clothes were all tarnished with ashes and soot;
A bundle of toys he had flung on his back,
And he looked like a peddler just opening his pack.
His eyes, how they twinkled! His dimples how merry!
His cheeks were like roses, his nose like a cherry!
His droll little mouth was drawn up like a bow,
And the beard of his chin was as white as the snow;

The stump of a pipe he held tight in his teeth,
And the smoke it encircled his head like a wreath;
He had a broad face and a little round belly,
That shook, when he laughed like a bowlful of jelly.
He was chubby and plump, a right jolly old elf,
And I laughed when I saw him, in spite of myself;
A wink of his eye and a twist of his head,
Soon gave me to know I had nothing to dread;

He spoke not a word, but went straight to his work,
And filled all the stockings; then turned with a jerk,
And laying his finger aside of his nose,
And giving a nod, up the chimney he rose;
He sprang to his sleigh, to his team gave a whistle,

And away they all flew like the down of a thistle.
But I heard him exclaim, as he drove out of sight,

**_"HAPPY CHRISTMAS TO ALL AND TO ALL A
GOOD-NIGHT."_**

## The Night Before Christmas

By the time Mark and Susie and Glenda and George made it over to T-Bone's Place for the night, most of the residents were in their rooms asleep. Nurse Vicky was still awake, as was Miguel and Cracker Jack Henderson.

"There's a pot of sassafras tea on the stove," Vicky said. "It'll make for sweet dreams."

Susie and Glenda helped themselves to steaming mugs full. "I don't think I dream," George said, getting comfortable in Steven's recliner.

"That's because you're too busy snoring," Glenda said.

Cracker Jack stared out the window. "I don't know how much more of this we can handle before...."

George glanced at him. "Don't worry. The generator's all ready to go if the power goes out. Everything'll be okay."

Mark threw his blankets and pillow on the floor and laid down. *A Christmas Carol* was playing on the television.

"I think this is probably my favorite Holiday movie," Susie said.

Vicky nodded. "Mine too. It's not religious, and yet it captures the spirit of Christmas like none other."

"I like *It's a Wonderful Life*," Cracker Jack said.

Glenda sipped her tea. "I don't. George annoys me."

George cocked an eyebrow. "You're talking about George Bailey, right?"

Another sip of tea. "Every time he starts whining, I want to scream."

"I'm glad we're not watching it then," Cracker Jack said. "He whines a lot."

"My favorite Christmas movie is *Miracle on 34th Street*." Miguel said. "That woman look just like my mama. When she smile, I cry."

Susie raised her hand. "Shhhh.... Here comes my favorite part."

*"I will honor Christmas in my heart and try to keep it all year. I will live in the past, the present, and the future."*

"This make me cry too," Miguel said.

*"The spirits of all three shall strive within me. I will not shut out the lessons that they teach."*

"I hope he keep his promise," Miguel said.

"It says he does."

Mark burrowed down under his covers. "You know this is fiction, right?"

"Be quiet."

*"I don't know what to do! I am as light as a feather, I am as happy as an angel; I am as merry as a school-boy."*

"I love how he dances and gets dizzy."

*"I am as giddy as a drunken man. A Merry Christmas to everybody! A happy New Year to all the world!"*

"Bet it doesn't last."

George appeared to be asleep. "Humbug."

*"And it was always said of him, that he knew how to keep Christmas well, if any man alive possessed the knowledge. May that be truly said of all of us!"*

"Yes."

*"God bless us,"* Tiny Tim said. *"Every One!"*

~ * ~

Gordon took the patrol officer's advice and tucked himself in behind a semi and for well over sixty miles had been gripping the steering wheel so tightly the discomfort in his arms had progressed from a dull ache to extreme pain, which was apparently just a precursor to their now going numb. He hadn't given any thought as to how to go about *not* following the truck and had been following so closely even when there was a turn-off or a rare service station, by the time he saw it he was past it.

He's stopped listening to the radio, it was a distraction, and hadn't even been able to take a drink of water or eat one of the snack bars he'd bought back when he gassed up the car because that would mean taking his hands off the wheel. He went through a period of talking to himself, not realizing he was practically hypnotizing himself by staring at the semi's taillights, and the sound of his own voice startled him on more than one occasion.

All that was bad enough, now he had to pee.

He glanced at his navigation screen. "Man-up," he told himself. "Reach quick and press the button. Just do it."

Such an accomplishment.

"I did it! Jackie?"

"Yes, Gordon. What can I do for you?"

"Can you tell me where the next service station is?"

"I will do my best." There was a short pause. "Sorry. I am detecting your general vicinity but...."

Gordon kept his hands firmly on the wheel, eyes glued to the semi's taillights.

"I am assuming you are wanting a station that is open?"

"Yessss...."

"Well, that seems to be a problem. I'm having a hard time pinpointing your route. Where are you?"

Gordon stared straight ahead, the snow coming down so hard at the moment the semis taillights were a blur. He wondered if he was dreaming. Have I fallen asleep? Am I in a ditch somewhere? "Where am I? Uh...I was hoping you'd tell me."

"You are heading North. That I can tell you, but...."

"Are you saying there are no service stations open?"

"No, I'm saying I can't detect where you are. By the way, you are not supposed to be on the road. There is a snow ban in effect."

"Well, that's nice to know, but I *am* on the road, and I'm a good two, three, or four hours away, depending on where the hell I'm at."

"Wait. There's a beacon."

"What?"

"A signal. It appears you are maybe ten minutes or so from Erie."

"Well, that's good news."

"Yes, but you could also be ten minutes past it. With the signal obscured it is hard to tell."

"Jackie, are you being paid double-time for the Holiday, because if so...."

"I can understand your frustration, Gordon."

"No, Jackie, you can't. I gotta piss like a racehorse and I'm following a semi and I can't see and you can't tell me where I'm at.... Wait a minute. Wait a minute. Did you hear what I just said? I said I have to piss like a racehorse. Where the hell did that come from?"

"I have no idea, Gordon."

A tunnel of darkness appeared and Gordon found himself studying the truck lights so hard, he thought he saw one side of them blinking. Or were they blinking? "The taillights are blinking."

"Your taillights? How can that be, Gordon?"

"I don't know. But they are. I'm gonna follow them."

"Be careful now, Gordon."

"You too, Jackie."

"Merry Christmas."

"Thank you. Oh, and Jackie, can you call my Mom and tell her I'm coming home."

"It'll be my pleasure."

"Do you need her number?" Gordon put on his blinker and followed the semi off the road.

"No, Gordon. I already have it. Good-bye."

~ * ~

Ben stirred in his sleep. "Meg."

"Yes."

"Where have you been?"

"I was checking on the children. It's so wonderful having them all here. I checked on everyone. That's what took me so long. They're all asleep. Even the dogs are asleep."

Ben smiled. "Come back to bed. It's been a long day."

Meg took off her slippers and snuggled up close.

"We had your lasagna for dinner."

"I know. We always have lasagna for Christmas Eve."

"Our family is very big on tradition."

"Our family. I love that. I love them."

"They know you're here."

"Of course, they do."

"Mr. Miller, you know it's no secret I wanted children."

"I know. So did I."

"And now they're everywhere. I have so many children I don't know what to do."

Ben chuckled,

"The power was out."

51

"Was it?" The room seemed so bright.

"It's back on now."

Ben heard the humming sound of the generator. "Remember when the power would go out and we would freeze our butts off."

"I don't remember it that way. I remember you always keeping me warm."

Ben tucked her in tighter, closer, holding on to the memories...even in his sleep.

"Good night, Mr. Miller."

"Good night, Meg."

"Merry Christmas."

~ * ~

Virtually no one other than Señor noticed the power was out. They were all bundled up and sound asleep. Even the children...especially the children, who were sleeping like little lambs nestled next to their mothers and fathers. Senior loaded more logs onto the fire and quietly put on his boots, jacket, hat, and gloves, and went out to start up the generator.

Randy woke when he heard the sound of the utility room door close behind him and just lay there, listening for a few minutes, then got up and went to check on him. He opened the door. "Are you okay, Dad? You need help?" he could see the flashlight in his father's hand, but not much else.

"No, I'm good."

No sooner said, the generator started up and Randy waited for his father to come back inside and whisked the snow off his jacket. "How much snow do you think we got?" Randy asked, barely above a whisper.

"At least three feet and no sign of letting up. I checked radar on my phone just before I went out. It's going to continue snowing all day. Go back to sleep, son."

Randy nodded and peered out the kitchen window. It was like looking into a thick white cloud. "Do you think they know over at T-Bone's that the power's out?"

"Yeah. They had their generator going before me. I'll never hear the end of it from George."

Randy smiled and patted his father on the back. "Good night, Dad."

~ * ~

When Tom's cellphone lit up in the night, he grabbed it quickly and stared at the screen. It was a text from Gordon.

"I'm off the road. Stuck."

Tom leaned away from Wendy and tried to focus on the tiny keyboard on his phone. "Where?" he texted.

"I don't know. Close, I think. Maybe about a mile or more, maybe less."

Tom sat up as quietly as he could so as not to wake Wendy. "What road?"

"I'm not sure."

When Tom tried to stand up, his knee buckled and he almost fell over. "Shit," he hissed.

Wendy rolled over. "What's going on?"

"Nothing. I just gotta go potty."

"Potty?"

"The kids are all around. Shhh...."

Wendy laughed softly and nestled down under the covers and fell back asleep.

Tom made it almost to the door before he heard a voice calling to him. "Pssst. Where you goin'?"

It was Junior.

Tom motioned outside.

"Wait up."

Speaking barely above a whisper, once they stepped outside and could actually talk, the gale force winds and frigid temperature all but took their breath away. "Get in my truck," Tom yelled, covering his face.

"Yeah, right! Where is it?"

"How the hell do I know? Look!"

Junior shielded his eyes and pointed. "Straight ahead."

Together they trudged through what was now close to four feet of snow, covering their faces and leaning into the wind.

"Holy shit! I've never seen this much snow in my life!"

When they reached the truck, Tom had to beat on the door to get it to open and climbed in only long enough to start it, turn on the defrost, and grab the snow scraper. Junior, for his part, was trying to clear the side windows as best he could and worked his way around to the taillights and back up around to clean off the headlights as Tom chipped away at the ice formed on the windshield under the heavy wet snow.

"I hate the snow!"

"No you don't!"

"I do now!"

"Go on! Get in!"

They shook the snow off as best they could, with it falling even harder now and sat inside shivering until the truck started to warm up.

"Where are we going?" Junior asked.

Tom had to laugh. "I gotta tell you, your blind trust in me is touching."

"Yeah, yeah, so what? Where are we going?"

Tom turned on the windshield wipers and cringed as they struggled to do some good. "Gordon's in a ditch about a mile from here. We're gonna go find him."

"A mile where?"

Tom put his truck into four-wheel drive. "Well, that'll be the tricky part. We have to try and find out. Get him on the phone. He's the most recent call."

Junior glanced at him and rolled his eyes. "In the middle of the night, I would think so."

Gordon answered on the first ring.

"We're leaving the farm now. Maybe...." Junior said.

"What do you mean maybe?"

Tom's truck sat spinning its tires, then finally dug in.

"Just kidding. Well, maybe not kidding, just...."

Tom smacked him on the arm. "Quit. He's probably scared to death as it is."

"He's not scared. He's a grown man. Gordon, are you scared?"

"Why? Should I be? Why are you asking me that?"

"Oh, just making conversation."

"Ask him if he has his headlights on?"

"He can hear you, Tom. I have him on speaker phone."

"Gordon, do you have your headlights on?"

"Probably. But I'm kinda nose down in the ditch, so...."

"Did you go past Pekin Road?"

"I think so. I might be just beyond the turn. That's when I started sliding. I slid for quite a distance."

"Put your window down on the off side," Junior said.

"The off side?"

"The other side of where the wind is blowing, and turn your radio on as loud as you can stand it. I'll listen for it."

Tom glanced at Junior. "Have you done this before?"

"In the dark? Yes. In the snow? No."

The road looked as if it had been plowed at least once, a narrow one-swipe pass that was barely visible, and a snow-pile embankment blocking the end of the driveway.

"I can't see either way, can you?"

"No. Go for it."

Tom held the wheel tight and gunned the engine, plowed through the snow, and did a complete donut turnaround out on the road.

"It's that way," Junior said, laughing.

Tom gave him a look.

"Come on, why would he be coming from any other direction?"

They crept down the road, both squinting and with the windshield wipers on high.

"Oh shit," Junior said, every time they started slipping and sliding. "Gordon, you still there?"

"Yes."

"I'll let you know when we get close."

"Okay."

"By the way, you don't need the music that loud yet."

"Oh, so now you tell me."

"Listen," Tom said, rolling his window down and then putting it right back up again. "Did you hear that?"

"Uh...."

Tom put his window down again, but only for a second.

"I hear it," Junior said.

"Is that as loud as it goes?"

The volume practically drowned Gordon out. "Yes. I think I hear something. I'll get out."

"No, don't!" Tom said. "In case we start sliding too, you're safer inside your car."

Junior nodded. "Good thinking, old man. Did you hear that, Gordon?"

"I heard it."

"Keep playing the radio."

"I think I see your lights."

Junior put his window down. "I hear your radio. I think." He covered the phone and leaned closer to the open window.

Tom slid to a stop at the corner, both listening.

"I think he's over there."

"I am," Gordon said. "I see you. I'm over here."

"Press your brake a couple times," Tom said.

"Yes!" Junior pointed. "There he is, over there."

Ben woke to see Meg looking out the kitchen window, her face illuminated by the twinkling of the colorful Christmas tree lights. She either couldn't sleep or he was dreaming, because she was just in the bedroom a minute ago, wrapped in his arms. He saw himself standing next to her and had to wonder.

"That's a lot of snow," she said.

Ben looked out the window.

"It's going to be such a nice day. I love the snow."

"I know."

Meg looked at him. "Do you remember our Charlie Brown Christmas tree?"

Ben chuckled. "How could I forget? That was the most pathetic tree I'd ever seen."

"At first," Meg said. "But then...."

"With time, and the way the branches sagged, it was beautiful."

57

Ben put his arm around her shoulders.

"I'm looking forward to everyone being here."

"Me too. I'm happy you're going to be here."

Meg smiled. "I'm always here, Mr. Miller. I told you that. I'm always right there where you are."

"But not like this. You're real."

Meg drew a breath and glanced over her shoulder. "Dawn's dreaming."

"Am I dreaming too?"

"No, at the moment just Dawn. She's dreaming she's five years old and she's so happy. She hasn't a care in the world."

They both looked at her with such love and admiration. She had Maeve tucked next to her on one side and D.R. on the other. Randy was sleeping close by, one arm draped over his eyes, the other across his chest. "They have a good marriage."

Ben nodded.

"Someone tended to the fire," Meg said.

"I see that."

"It's nice and cozy."

Ben looked around the room. The house never looked so big before, a place for everyone.

"I love the Holidays," Meg said. "I always have and I always will."

Ben smiled and adjusted his pillow. "I know."

~ * ~

Gordon's car had ended up in a ditch at least ten feet off the road. Tom walked around it as best he could, thigh deep in snow and trying to shield his eyes from the wind.

58

"We'll come back tomorrow and get it when the snow stops. Get what you need out of it. Come on, let's go."

"We're just going to leave it?"

"Yes. It's fine. No one's going to try and come steal it in this weather and it's too far off the road to hit. Go on, get your stuff. I'll be in the truck."

Gordon looked at Junior, shoulders hunched and chewing gum. "I don't want my jaw to freeze," Junior said.

"Do you think we should just leave it?"

"Is it insured?"

Gordon nodded. "Of course."

"Then yeah, why not? Leave it. Do you need help with your shit?"

"No, it's just a carry-on."

Hearing that, Junior turned and made his way up the hill out of the ditch to Tom's truck. Gordon followed, dragging his carry-on luggage through the snow.

Junior opened the door. "Throw it in the back."

Gordon tossed it over Junior's shoulder into the extended compartment. "Should I leave a note in case the cops come?"

"If you want," Tom said.

"You got anything for me to write on?"

Tom just looked at him for a second.

"My bag's packed solid."

Tom motioned to his glove compartment. "Look in there."

Junior searched inside and found a folded piece of paper. "Wait a minute, tell me you paid this?" It was a speeding ticket.

"Uh...."

Gordon looked up at the two of them, snow blowing all around. "Isn't there anything else? Come on, I'm freezing."

Junior rummaged through the glove compartment. "Here, how about this one."

Tom squinted and read the date. "Now that one I paid, I'm pretty sure. Use that one."

Junior handed it to Gordon along with a pen and after pulling the door shut, watched Gordon stumble and fall his way down the hill into the ditch and back up again. "I'll bet he's one hell of a skier."

Tom laughed.

Gordon climbed up into the truck, his nose dripping, teeth chattering, and eyes watering. "My feet are froze solid."

Tom and Junior glanced at his soaking wet shoes; wingtips.

"Don't you have any boots?" Junior asked.

"Yes," Gordon said, shivering. "I left them at the farm."

"Well, had I known...." Tom said, with that ornery grin of his.

Gordon looked at him, absorbing the humor, but too cold for a comeback. "Pop, can we just go home now?"

Tom nodded, and halfway down the road, glanced at him and Junior, two complete opposites, close in age, and just shook his head. One grew up how a kid shouldn't have to and turned out to be a good man, finally. And the other, having lost his father at a young age, though now a convert to city life, braved the storm of the century to come home and be with his family for Christmas. "If I never say this again, to both of you or either one of you for that matter, I want you to know I'm proud of you. I'm proud of you both."

Neither Gordon nor Junior knew what to say. They both just nodded and stared straight ahead into the almost blinding snow as they slowly followed the path home to Meg's Meadows.

## *Christmas Morning*

Ashley, the youngest member of the family woke first and Maria, Maeve, Julie, and D.R. soon followed, jumping up and down and squealing.

"It's Christmas!"

"It's Christmas!"

"Santa Claus came!"

"Santa Claus was here!"

The aroma of coffee brewing beckoned the adults.

"What's all this noise about?" Ben said, coming down the hall.

"Santa Claus came, Grandpa! Look!"

"Well, I see he did indeed. I guess it must really be Christmas then!"

"It is, Grandpa! It is!"

Wendy poured Ben a cup of coffee and glanced out the kitchen window. There had to be at least four or five feet of snow on the ground, maybe more. No way Gordon could make it through this much snow. She hoped wherever he was that he was safe and sound, and said a silent prayer hoping he wasn't alone on this Christmas day.

"Mom, pour me a cup," she heard someone say. She turned. Matthew didn't drink coffee. He drank tea.

"Gordon?"

Her son smiled; that same sleepy smile from when he was a little boy, now a grown man.

"Oh my God, you made it."

"Thanks to Pop and Junior."

Junior opened a sleepy eye and rolled onto his side.

Wendy gave Ben his coffee and rushed over to hug her son. "It's Christmas! It's Christmas after all!"

The children looked at her. "Can we open our gifts now?"

"Yes!" Wendy said. "Yes!"

In the ensuing chaos, the dogs were let out, the dogs were let back in, and Mark and Susie came in along with George and Glenda.

"The horses are all okay. We just fed them."

"How long has the power been out?"

"Nine hours."

"The generators working okay?"

"Yep!"

Ben passed out sticks of licorice, congratulating everyone for surviving the storm, and each child received one large gift from Santa Claus and three smaller ones. They tore through the wrapping paper, with the slightly-though-wiped-off wet dogs all around them, snatching the paper and crinkling it and shredding it to bits.

"Gimpy! Gimpy, gimmee that!"

"Get that from him!"

Ben laughed. Chaos indeed. "What did you get?"

"Look, Grandpa. A Winky Doll!" Maria said.

"I got one too," Maeve said.

"I got a Pixie Pony!" Julie said.

Ashley just giggled, holding up a talking Monkey with the paws of a lion, the color of a tiger, and a child's voice that sounded just like her. "I luv it!"

"What did you just say?"

"I luv it!"

"I luv it!"

Everyone laughed. Apparently, it had a voice recorder inside which immediately played back what a child had just said. "I luv it!"

D.R. sat quietly enamored with his gift.

"What is it?"

"It's a Space Recorder." D.R. looked at his father. "How did Santa Claus know?"

"Santa Claus knows everything," Randy said.

"But I didn't tell him. I kept it to myself."

"Well, somebody must have known."

Carol smiled. He'd purposely not told anyone, a test of sorts to see if Santa was truly real or not, but she knew. "A good nanny always knows," she said of many occasions over the years.

The adults always participated in a gift exchange where names were drawn, and a strict twenty-dollar limit. The only stipulation being, it had to be something they felt the person would want or needed. The gifts and the reactions were always entertaining.

Cindy got a foot massager for her swollen feet. "Thank you! Thank you!" Linda got a white-noise maker. She was always saying how she could hear Señor snoring from all the way down the hall. Randy got a coffee mug guaranteed to keep coffee hot for up to twenty-four hours. Coincidently, Mark got one of those too, though a different color. Dawn received a journal. Yes, it was time for her to start writing again. Liz got a book-sized magnifying glass. Ben got a new stopwatch. Señor received a rice-hull neck pillow. Marvin got a video game, an obsession of his. Gordon got a compass. His mother had drawn his name and wanted him to always know the way home. Hillary received a sundial, Wendy, a single serving ice crusher. She loved crushed ice. Tom got a new pair of reading glasses. The ones he had now were taped in three different places. Glenda got a winter herb garden kit. George received an Emmylou Harris CD. "Oh yeah!" It was the only one he didn't have. Dusty got a back brace. His back had been bothering him quite a bit lately.

Matthew received an artist's apron. Junior got a new belt buckle. Lucy had the word Daddy engraved on it. Carol got an advanced-level crossword puzzle book and Susie got a lava lamp.

Strata had been made yesterday for breakfast this morning and needed only to be heated and was served with cinnamon rolls, fruit salad, and the children's favorite; oatmeal cookies with nuts, dark chocolate, and raisins.

"It's Christmas!"

The children ate at the kid's table, most everyone else either ate where they'd slept or at the dining room table, and for all practical purposes it was an indoor picnic, paper plates and all. Old Man Jackson, Karen, and Veronica were enjoying the same scrumptious Christmas morning breakfast at Shifting Gears, as were Nurse Vicky and the residents at T-Bone's Place. It was still snowing.

~ * ~

Old Man Jackson forged his way to the barn holding on to the anchor rope he'd tied to guide the way. Karen and Veronica, all bundled up, huddled behind him. Jackson glanced back. Karen had fallen and just lay there for a moment, laughing in the snow. Her voice sounded like a child's on a playground during recess at school.

Veronica fussed and fretted over her. "Are you okay? Here, let me help you up."

Karen batted her hands away. "I'm fine! I'm fine! Oh God, that was fun," she said, pulling herself to her feet. Not two seconds later, Old Man Jackson fell and he too couldn't help but laugh. He literally was sitting in a snowbank.

"Do you need help?" Karen asked, still laughing.

"No, just some momentum. Here I go, one two...."
When he fell back again, all three of them laughed. "It's like trying to stand up after sitting on a cloud."

Karen and Veronica climbed their way through the snow to get behind him and each gave him a shove, which almost sent him falling in the other direction.

"Okay," he said, still laughing. "Let's all grab ahold of the rope and move on. Here we go."

It would take all three of them to pry the barn door open. The piled-up drifting snow blocked the path on one end and the ice dam from the melting snow from the animal's warmth, jammed the other. After some considerable pushing and shoving and pounding, finally...they stepped inside to what looked and felt like a cocoon, ice crystals glittering the walls. The horses nickered, safe and sound, oblivious to the blizzard and eager for their breakfast.

"Merry Christmas, children!" Karen said. "It's a beautiful morning!"

Veronica glanced at Old Man Jackson and rolled her eyes. "She's forever sunshine. It's so annoying."

Jackson watered the horses, Karen hayed them, Veronica grained them, and less than fifteen minutes later, they were making their way back to the house. No falling this time, no laughing. The snowfall had intensified. They leaned into the blinding snow, gripping the guide rope, and kept their heads down. Christmas dinner was warming on the cooktop of their wood burner with a delicious aroma to help lead the way, and though it appeared the worst of the storm thus far was upon them, all was abundantly well.

~ * ~

The old-timers at T-Bone's Place were looking forward to Christmas dinner as well, warm and snug, generator humming, as they watched the movie White Christmas starring Bing Crosby, Danny Kaye, Rosemary Clooney, and Vera-Ellen.

"I think this movie was originally in black and white," Clint said.

"No. It's always been in color." Steven said. "They're not that old."

Jeannie glanced at them. "Not that old? They're all dead."

"All of them?"

"All of them."

"That's a shame." Frank said. "I like this movie."

"Why is that a shame?"

"Because, you just said they're all dead."

Vicky laughed from in the kitchen.

"I smell turkey." Bill said.

"No, you smell the stuffing and gravy," Vicky said.

"It smells like turkey."

"That's because of the turkey gravy and giblets in the stuffing."

"You mean we aren't going to have turkey?"

"No, the turkey's being smoked. It'll be done soon."

"I don't think I've ever had a smoked turkey before."

"Yes, you did. Just last year."

"And the year before that, and the year before that," Frank said.

"Did I like it?"

"You had three helpings."

"I guess I liked it then."

This was right about the time the stars in the movie started singing the title song, and everyone at T-Bone's sang along.

I'm Dreaming of a White Christmas
Just like the ones I used to know
Where the treetops glisten and children listen
To hear sleigh bells in the snow

I'm dreaming of a white Christmas
With every Christmas card I write
May your days be merry and bright
And may all your Christmases be white!

"Merry Christmas!"

~ * ~

With dinner already prepared and the turkeys in the smoker, the morning at Meg's Meadows was spent simply enjoying Christmas and the added bonus of having everyone home and all under one roof. The children played non-stop with their new toys and when they asked if they could wear their pajamas all day, the answer was a resounding yes.

"You can wear them until we're all allowed outside again," Liz said.

"That could be days, or weeks, or..." D.R. said, listening to his Space Recorder.

"More like days." Cindy was still in her pajamas as well. Pajamas, socks, slippers, and robe curled up in front of the fire. "Is it time to eat yet?"

Ben had nodded off several times in his easy chair. Dusty was thinking about a nap. Linda, Dawn, Carol, Susie, and Lucy were all working on a jigsaw puzzle. Glenda was reading a book. Hillary was doing her yoga stretches. Liz was crocheting a scarf. Tom, Señor, Matthew, Gordon, Randy, George and Mark were playing cards. And the dogs were stretched out here, there, and everywhere.

Ashley was learning to recognize each of them and say their names.

"Gimpy."

"No, that's Sloopy," Marvin said. "They look alike, but...."

"Who's that?"

"Runt."

"Yes."

"And this one?"

"Dawber," she said, pronouncing it Dobbler.

Tom cleared his throat. "You sure? That looks like Boogie Boogie to me."

Ashley laughed. "Uncle Tom! There's no Boogie Boogie."

"Really?"

"And who's that?"

"Piccolo."

Liz looked up from crocheting without missing a stitch and smiled. "I love how she pronounces Piccolo. It sounds a little like peekieboo."

"Where's Rotty?"

"I don't know." Ashley looked around the room. "Rotty. Rotty. Where did he go? There he is." The dog was lying near Dusty's chair.

"He's been sticking to me like glue lately," Dusty said.

"Since the snow started?" Mark asked.

"No, even before that. Ever since I...."

"What?"

"Nothing. Never mind. It's just been the last couple of weeks."

Ben looked at him. "Ever since...?"

"Since I fell."

"When?"

"A couple of weeks ago."

"Where?"

"Down the stairs."

"Did you get hurt?"

"Just a little. I got over it."

"Shit, I'd be playing it up if it were me," Junior said. "Look at all the mileage George got when he fell. Ooh, I can't walk. Ooh, I can't dance."

George looked at him. "Hey, as a rule I don't dance either way. Okay? Get your story straight."

Junior laughed.

"Seriously," Ben said. "Why didn't you say something?"

Dusty shrugged. "I didn't want to be a bother."

"Since when?" Tom asked.

"Oh, since I think I'm becoming one."

"What do you mean?"

"The stairs. I love the loft, I love being there, but...."

Gordon held up his hand. "If you're thinking of vacating it, I want it."

Everyone looked at him.

"Just letting you know," he added sheepishly.

Tom turned to Dusty. "Are you saying the stairs are getting too hard for you?"

"Yes," Hillary said. "That's exactly what he's saying."

Everyone looked at her now.

"Rotty senses it."

Gordon started to say something but hesitated.

"Have you seen a doctor?" Randy asked.

"No. I took some Bute."

Randy lowered his head and sighed.

"And some Bactrim."

"Alrighty then." Mark laid his cards down. "Gin."

"You sneak," Junior said.

"What? I can't help it if you don't know how to play cards."

"Dusty, you can stay with us till your back gets better," Susie said.

Mark nodded, agreeing.

"Nah, I don't think it's going to get better. I'd put my name on the list at T-Bone's if I weren't afraid of jinxing someone into moving along sooner than anticipated. But frankly, I think my days of going up and down the stairs two and three times a day are over."

"So, move in here," Ben said. "Take the spare room."

"Well, then it wouldn't be a spare room anymore now would it. What happens when that room's needed?"

"Uh...." Gordon interrupted. "That's what's I was going to say. Don't worry about me needing it. I'm going to try and find a place for when...."

"That's silly," Wendy said. "Why would you rent a place only to use it once or twice a year? Besides, this isn't exactly a sublet or timeshare area."

"I know that. But I'm thinking I want to move home, only I want a place of my own."

"For good?"

"For a while at least, to see how it goes. I've got all my things in my car in the ditch. My clothes, my computer, everything. I can work remotely."

"I'll hook you up," Marvin said. "How fast do you want your internet to be?"

"Wait a minute." Wendy smiled. "You're moving home?"

"Yes, Mom. I'm moving home."

"Now?"

"Yes.. It's now or never."

Wendy jumped up and hurried over to give him a big hug.

"Mom, stop! You're smothering me!"

Matthew looked at the two of them and smiled. "Welcome home, Brother."

~ * ~

Another six inches of snow accumulated by noon with no sign of letting up. Plumes from the smoker blended with the blowing snow, blurring Señor's vision as he checked the pop-up thermometers on the Christmas turkeys.

George stuck his head out the doorway. "Are they done?"

"Just about. A few more minutes."

George put on his jacket and hat and came outside. You could see their breath as they hovered close to the cookers. "I love the smell of hickory smoke."

"You love the smell of turkey."

"Yeah, that too."

Señor glanced at him, shielding his eyes from a snowy wind gust. "Is everything ready?"

"Yep, just waiting for the turkeys."

"That one right there will be done first, right about...." Señor paused. "Now."

George leaned down to see for himself.

"The others will be done in about five to eight minutes."

"You've got it down to a science."

Señor shrugged. "Get me that first roaster. They're just inside the door on the right."

George marveled as he reached inside for it. The other two were lined up right behind it. "Do you ever mess up, Señor? I mean really mess up?"

"Oh sure. But I'd have to give some thought as to when." He and George laughed. It was hard to imagine the two of them not getting along so well, but once upon a time it was true. George held the roasting pan while Señor lifted the turkey out of the smoker. "Take this one to T-Bone's."

"How do you know which one is theirs?"

Señor smiled. "They're all the same. Taking them theirs first will get you back here just in time for the other ones." George carried the roaster over to the Gator, loaded it and climbed behind the wheel. Señor had already plowed the path several times that morning but the heavy snow continued to fall. "Plow as you go. It'll save me going back out again."

George lowered the plow and off he went. The hum of the gator pushing snow sounded almost like a whisper. Señor looked around. It was a winter wonderland; the barns covered in snow, the fence rails and posts piled high, the houses.... He laughed. Though far away, the lights at T-Bone's Place shown bright and he could see someone standing watch in every window. There was no mistaking Cracker Jack Henderson when he raised his arms in jubilation, that crazy wild hair of his like a halo around his head. Señor could imagine his saying "Here comes the turkey!" He smiled as the snow pelted his face. "Yes, here it comes!"

~ * ~

At precisely that same moment several miles away, Old Man Jackson was placing *their* smoked turkey on the table. It had been warmed precisely as Señor had instructed, "Not too hot, don't serve it cold, serve it just right. Let it sit for ten minutes."

"Will you do the honors, Jackson?" Karen asked.

Jackson smiled and ceremoniously raised the carving knife and fork. "Don't mind if I do. Dark meat or white?"

"Both," Karen and Veronica said in unison.

The kitchen was toasty warm, the aroma delicious. When the turkey was carved and Jackson took his seat across from them, Veronica asked if he'd like to say grace.

Jackson stared down at his plate.

"A blessing," she added, when he appeared reluctant or perhaps confused by the request. "For we are indeed blessed on this fine day."

Veronica looked from one to the other. "See. I told you, always sunshine."

Jackson drew a breath and sighed. "A blessing. Well, let me see. Since the Lord above might just be listening, I want to say I'm blessed to be here with both of you. Lord, I thank you. Amen."

"Wait!" Karen said when Jackson raised his fork to dig in. "We got you a gift."

"A gift? I'm sorry, I didn't...."

Karen hurried to one of the kitchen cabinets and returned with a small mason jar of clear liquid with a pretty red bow tied around the lid. "From us to you."

Jackson took the jar and smiled. "Why, thank you. Thank you very much."

Karen nodded proudly. "That's your gift to us."

Jackson glanced from one to the other, two strange and eccentric women, one as goofy as the other in her own way and yet with hearts of pure gold.

"Your gift to us is your acceptance for who we are. Thank you."

"You're welcome." Jackson smiled. "Uh, can we eat now?"

"Yes. Merry Christmas!"

~ * ~

The landline phone at Meg's Meadows rang again with an updated weather bulletin. "A foot or more additional snow is forecast in the Lake Effect snowbelt. Power outages are expected to take days and possibly weeks to restore. All parking bans are in effect until further notice. Highway Patrol asks that you stay off the roads. Emergency vehicles only."

Tom looked at Gordon. "We'll take the tractor and get your car tomorrow. That's if we can see where we're going."

Gordon nodded. "I doubt we'll be able to find it."

"There's always the spring thaw," Matthew said.

"Oh, and you think that's funny?"

Junior laughed. "You might want to think about trading that car in on a real vehicle. You know, like a truck. A four-wheel drive truck."

"With all that blowing snow and no visibility, are you trying to say I wouldn't have slid off the road if I'd been driving a truck."

"Well, not necessarily. But if you recall, we got to you and back in one without any problem, so...."

They all laughed, and with that, even Gordon had to laugh.

"You sure you want to move home?"

"Yes," Gordon said, without hesitating. "Yes."

"Dinner's ready!" Liz announced.

The table had been set with Meg's *good dishes*, which is what she used to call them. Even the children got a big plate. When they all took their seats and the customary Holiday dinner photos were taken of the feast. "Look this way, lean back, okay everyone smile, say cheese." It was finally time for the children to reveal their surprise.

"Instead of a prayer," Carol said.

"We wrote a song!" D.R. could hardly contain himself. He'd kept the secret for so long....

"We all wrote it," Maria said.

"And we signed it," Maeve added. "We signed languaged the whole song."

Ashley and Julie nodded emphatically.

Carol lined them up by size, put Ashley on a stool, and drew a deep breath. "Are we ready?" Everyone looked on with anticipation, phone cameras in hand as the children cradled their arms as if holding a baby.

~ Baby Jesus, Baby Jesus ~
~ It's your birthday today ~

The children rocked the baby Jesus and touched their fingers to the palms of their hands as they sang.

~ Baby Jesus, Baby Jesus ~
~ Today of all days ~

Ben smiled. Meg was standing behind them, signing as well, and so happy.

~ We will always remember; we will never forget ~
~ Baby Jesus, Baby Jesus, the day we first met ~

The children touched their foreheads, and then shook one another's hands.

~ You bring promise, you bring love ~
~ You show us the way ~

When the children touched their hearts as the sign for love, the adults around the table all had tears in their eyes.

~ Baby Jesus, Baby Jesus ~
~ It's your birthday today ~


There was a momentary silence after the children sang the last verse, all five of them looking on in anticipation, their darling little faces all lit up. Then everyone started clapping, even the children. They hugged one another and took a bow, then another bow, and then it was time to eat, to celebrate. Laid out before them indeed was a feast. Smoked turkey and stuffing, mashed potatoes and gravy, green bean casserole and candied sweet potatoes, rolls with melted honey butter. And for dessert later, there was apple pie, pumpkin pie, and double chocolate brownies.

Ben looked around the table at his family and smiled. Meg would have loved to have been there, and she was. She was in each and every one of them. She was in their hearts, and she was in his forevermore. As the snow fell even harder, there was warmth inside and abundance in love.

"I am blessed, Meg."

"So am I," she said. "So am I. I am loved and I thank you for that. Thank you for all these children. Thank you for our family. Thank you, Baby Jesus."

*From Meg's Meadows to You and Yours,*
*Merry Christmas!!*

Sunrise Horse Farm would like to thank you for making the Winning Odds Series such a big hit. You'll be happy to know Book Nine is already in the works. Please log onto amazon.com to post a review and let us know what you think. As Ben would say, "It'll be good to hear from you!" Happy Holidays!!

~ * ~

Sunrise Horse Farm is an organic farm and equine retirement sanctuary located in Northeast Ohio. It is home to a bevy of rescue dogs, seven retired Thoroughbred racehorses, 3 fillies, a colt and a Morgan mare with an attitude. Owned and operated by John & MaryAnn Myers, Sunrise Horse Farm is dedicated to publishing books with integrity. Bestselling author of the Winning Odds and Maple Dale Series, horse trainer, equestrian, and environmentalist, MaryAnn writes about what she knows and loves, horses! If she's not home on the farm, chances are you'll find her at the racetrack!

www.sunrisehorsefarm.com

Made in the USA
Lexington, KY
30 November 2019

57883389R00046